DIY CANNABIS EXTRACTS 101

The Essential And Easy Beginner's
Cannabis Cookbook On How To Make
Medical Marijuana Extracts At Home

Tommy Rosenthal

© **Copyright 2020** by Tommy Rosenthal – All rights reserved.

In no way is it legal to reproduce, duplicate, or transmit any part of this document in either electronic means or in printed format. Recording of this publication is strictly prohibited and any storage of this document is not allowed unless with written permission from the publisher.

The information provided herein is stated to be truthful and consistent, in that any liability, in terms of inattention or otherwise, by any usage or abuse of any policies, processes, or directions contained within is the solitary and utter responsibility of the recipient reader. Under no circumstances will any legal responsibility or blame be held against the author for any reparation, damages, or monetary loss due to the information herein, either directly or indirectly.

The information herein is offered for informational purposes solely, and is universal as so. The presentation of the information is without contract or any type of guarantee assurance.

The information contained in this book is for educational and general information purposes only. Any content contained in this book should not be considered advice or recommendations.

You should consider professional advice before applying any of the information contained in this book.

While every precaution has been taken in the preparation of this book, the publisher and author assume no responsibility for errors or omissions, or for damages resulting from the use of the information contained herein.

The author and publisher are not responsible for any loss caused, whether due to negligence or otherwise, resulting from the use of, or reliance on, the information in this book provided directly or indirectly.

MEDICAL DISCLAIMER: The information contained in this book is intended for general information purposes only. You should always see your physician, health care provider and/or cannabis extracts expert before administering any suggestions made in this book. Any application of the material set forth in the following pages is at your discretion and is your sole responsibility.

REVIEWS

Reviews and feedback help improve this book and the author.

If you enjoy this book, we would greatly appreciate it if you were able to take a few moments to share your opinion and post a review online.

Table of Contents

Introduction 6
Chapter One: A Brief History of Cannabis 10
Chapter Two: What Is A Cannabis Extract? 18
Chapter Three: Cannabis Extraction And Consistency 22
Chapter Four: Dabbing 32
Chapter Five: How To Make Kief 36
Chapter Six: How To Make Hash 42
Chapter Seven: How To Make Cannabutter 50
Chapter Eight: How To Make Rosin 56
Chapter Nine: How To Make Tinctures 60
Chapter Ten: How To Make RSO (Rick Simpson Oil) 66
Final Thoughts 72
BONUS CHAPTER: What Is CBD? 74
Did You Like This Book? 88
By The Same Author 89

Introduction

First of all, I want to congratulate and thank you for downloading this book. I hope that it fulfills everything that you expect it too. But the question is, what is that?

I'm assuming that you want to know more about cannabis extracts. You've heard the term, people have probably even told you a little about them and how good they are. Well now you want to find out for yourself if all the hype is true.

This book covers a few basics that will help you achieve this purpose. First it will introduce you to what extracts actually are and what they are used for. The idea is for this book to be for the beginner, so the explanations will be simple and easy to follow. Once that is all covered, it will then guide you through the process of making your own extracts.

The amazing thing about extracts are that the majority of them can be made at home with materials and tools that you most likely already possess. So, consider this book like that off a cook book; it shows you what the product is and then tells you how to make it. From basic kief all the way through the Butane Oil. It is all doable and all explained.

I have tried all these methods myself, many time for a particular few, and they all work. Although it should also be noted that like with any recipe the steps do need to be followed precisely. If you step out of the guidelines, don't be surprised when your yield is different to what was expected.

So, what are you waiting for? You have the book. You have the motivation (I assume you do as you bought the book in the first place) now all you need do is go out and make extracts of you own. To that, I say good luck.

Oh, and one final note. It should be stated that the use of weed as dictated by the book is strictly for medical use only. I don't condone the use of it recreationally.

Chapter One: A Brief History of Cannabis

Key Takeaway*: The use of the cannabis plant (hemp) for woven fabric dates back over 11,000 years ago. Its first recorded use of ingestion is in 2737 BC, when the Chinese Emperor advocated is as medication. Cannabis extracts have a shorter history, it only started in the late 20th century. However, it has seen a quick rise in popularity, especially among those interested in its medicinal qualities.*

The history of the cannabis plant is a long and interesting one that dates back well into pre-historical times. The hemp plants durability and ability to grow literally anywhere under any conditions is what has made it such a resilient product throughout history.

Cannabis: A Journey Through The Ages

It is believed that the first woven forms of fabric were in fact used from the hemp plant, over 11,000 years ago. But in terms of its actual ingestion, the first recorded use can be traced back to 2737 B.C.E. This first use was by the Chinese Emperor Shen Nung who advocated it as a medication for gout, malaria and rheumatism, among other things. Although it was also used for intoxication purposes, it was its medical proficiencies that were considered most important.

And indeed, marijuana has been used consistently by a range of different cultures across the globe for thousands of years, from the Egyptians who used it to treat glaucoma and inflammations, right on through to the Persians who listed it as one of the most important medical plants.

It didn't find its way into the white America's until its introduction to Jamestown in 1611. And even then it was regaled for its medical uses above its hallucinogenic properties. Cannabis enjoyed immense, and legal, popularity in America for several hundred years in fact. It wasn't until the 1930s that a taboo grew around it and even still, it wasn't until The Controlled Substance Act of 1970 that it became classed as a schedule 1 drug and became completely illegal across the board.

It might be argued that there has been a resurgence in the popularity of marijuana of late, especially where it pertains to its medical functions. Because at the end of the day, once you eliminate the recreational properties that marijuana is most popular for, it's also an amazing healer and can be used for a range of different medical purposes.

Cannabis As A Medical Treatment

As mentioned above, cannabis has been in use as a form of medicine since at least 2737 BC. In the U.S. especially, its medical properties are starting to be preached more and more regularly as more states move towards legalizing marijuana for both medical and recreational use.

It is generally believed that the cannabis plant has two active chemicals that can be harnessed for medical value. These are cannabidiol (CBD) and tetrahydrocannabinol (THC). CBD is believed to be able to impact the brain without inducing a high state where THC is believed to have the ability to reduce pain and inflammations. Together, and where properly applied, they can work wonders.

If you want to learn more about the powerful healing properties of CBD, check out my other book: CBD Hemp Oil 101. Next to THC, CBD is the other main cannabinoid in the cannabis plant. Unlike THC, CBD does not get you high. But, even though the scientific research on the effects of CBD is still in its early stages, it is already associated with a great number of positive health effects. Using CBD Hemp Oil can really change your life!

Let's get back to the topic of this book though. Examples of ailments that marijuana has been known to either cure or have a significant impact on include glaucoma, epilepsy, anxiety, Alzheimer's disease, multiple sclerosis and even some forms of cancer.

The reason that there are so many presumptions around medicinal marijuana, rather than cold hard facts, is due to its classification as a schedule 1 drug. Under law, drugs that fall into this category can't even be studied in order to confirm their medical benefits; at least not at the federal level.

But even so, most agree that its applications are endless and what's more, with the recent insurgence of cannabis extracts, these treatments are becoming readily available to more and more people.

A Brief History Of Extraction

Unlike cannabis itself, cannabis extracts have a very brief history. There are of course stories that have emerged from Word War II scientific experiments that utilized THC extraction for mind-bending experiments. And in 1937, the book 'Cannabis Alchemy: The Art of Modern Hashmaking,' was published. It gives a brief overview of how to make hash 'honey oil.' But it wasn't until well into the 1990s that extracting really took off.

The extracting boom is generally credited to the online psychoactive library Erowid which, in 1999, put out an article titled 'Hash Honey Oil Technique.' This was the first detailed description of using butane oil to extract hash oil. Although it was very dangerous and a little on the amateur side, it did give birth to what is now known as the 'closed loop system' of extraction.

I'm getting ahead of myself here, but as a preview of what is to come: a closed loop extraction is one in which butane is run over the marijuana plant, solvating the THC chemical from it. It then enters a collection chamber and evaporates the butane chemical, leaving you with a pure THC product, or 'extract.' This form of extraction is used across the board when it comes to butane extraction and is responsible for the rise in popularity of cannabis extracts.

So, what is a cannabis extract exactly? We'll look at that next!

Chapter Two: What Is A Cannabis Extract?

Key Takeaway: This chapter is for the absolute novice in cannabis and cannabis extracts. A cannabis extract is the result of 'extracting' the THC cannabinoid from the plant. What you are left with is a small, 'pure' piece of cannabis.

By now you've probably heard the term 'cannabis extract,' quite a few times in your life. You've probably also heard the terms 'cannabis concentrates,' 'dabs,' 'budder,' 'wax,' etc etc. The list goes on and on. Some of these are interchangeable terms, others not so much. It's time to lay out what a cannabis extract actually is.

Cannabis Extracts Explained

Extraction itself is a pretty common biological process used by biologists to create natural byproducts from different types of plants. What this essentially means is that they are harnessing the plant in its most pure form, doing away with the undesirable compounds while keeping the ones they need for research and other purposes. Now apply this to the cannabis plant.

Cannabis extraction is the process by which the cannabinoids of a cannabis plant (THC) and the terpenes (the compounds that create flavor) are extracted from the plant in their purest form. This is done using a range of different processes (see Chapters Five to Ten) leaving the extractor with a sample of cannabis that, when ingested, is far more potent than were it just smoked or used in a common fashion.

It should also be noted that a cannabis extract is the exact same thing as a cannabis concentrate. The two words are interchangeable. And that's it!

Why Extract?

Now that you know what a cannabis extract is, you might be wondering what the point is. Why not just use weed as mother nature intended?

From a medical point of view, extraction has significant advantages. The first is potency. The feeling that one gets from being high is a chemical reaction your brain goes through when introduced to the cannabinoid THC. Smoking a weed plant the regular way will yield the smoker roughly 15%-20% of the THC held in that cannabinoid. Now, compare that to an extract where the user can access as much as 94% of the THC per hit.

This is a huge increase that can have significant effects for people who rely on the drug for relief from pain and other physical maladies. For example, if you choose to eat instead of smoke the marijuana plant, you will have to wait up to an hour for the effects to be felt. Using an extract (such as tincture) will not only hit you faster, but it will be far more effective.

From a scientific standpoint too, the ability to harness the THC compound in what is essentially its pure form, allows for far more aggressive research into the healing properties of the plant. In short, cannabis extracts are paving the way for medical breakthroughs that would have been impossible if you would just use a regular cannabis plants.

And finally, for the recreational user, as an extract is that much stronger, you don't need that much for each session. This makes it a much more cost-effective way to get high.

Chapter Three: Cannabis Extraction And Consistency

Key Takeaway: *In this chapter I will expand on the two methods of extraction; solvent based and non-solvent based. These two processes result in very different extracts.*

The Two Forms of Extraction

The simplest way to talk about cannabis extraction is to divide it into the two different processes utilized to extract the cannabinoids from the plant. These two processes are known as solvent extractions and solvent-less extractions.

SOLVENTS

Solvent extractions use a chemical based solution to separate the cannabinoids and terpenes from the cannabis plant. Typical solvents include butane, propane, Co2 and alcohol. The result of this is what is usually referred to as 'oil.'

There are two main drawbacks to using solvent distractions. The first comes from the argument that, because of the use of chemicals, the resulting product isn't as pure or good for you as solvent-less distractions. Even though the THC concentrate is just as high, these extractions might not be advisable for the health concise.

The other drawback is that a solvent based extraction can be far more dangerous for someone doing the process at home. The use of butane is especially dangerous. That is why I don't recommend using that at home, and the process is not described in this book.

SOLVENT-LESS

A solvent-less extraction is a mechanical process by which the resins and trichomes of the cannabis plant are pressed out of the bud and stem using mechanical processes. These are often a lot drier and you'll usually here them referred to as hash or sift.

This method is preferred by a majority of users for two main reasons. The first is that it is believed to be the purest form of extraction and thus the one that is the best for you. As no chemicals are used during this process, what you are left with are pure trichome heads and terpenes, with no chemical induction. The THC purity is the same, depending on the form of extraction used, but the lack of chemicals is a big plus.

Secondly, the lack of chemicals used also makes this method far easier to perform by the home chemist. There is no danger involved in any of the methods (See Chapters Five, Six and Seven) and they are all relatively simple.

WHICH TO USE?

Ultimately there is no 'better' or 'worse,' kind when it come to your personal high. That is usually a personal preference. When people do talk about the type of extract that they prefer, they are more often than not talking about the type of 'consistency,' that they like; not the extraction process itself.

The Consistencies Of Concentrates

Ultimately, when you hear people talking about what type of cannabis concentrate they like to use, they won't be talking about the solvents that were used to extract (only the more hardcore users will know this information). What they are often talking about is the consistency and texture of the extract. You may have heard terms like 'wax,' 'oil,' or 'crumble.' These are all extracts, interchangeable in use, but not in design.

One thing that you really need to be aware of too, is that the type of solvent used to extract the THC doesn't always have an effect on the consistency. Say for example that butane oil is used to extract. This in itself can be turned into either shatter, oil or budder. It just depends on the person making it and what they prefer.

Below is a list and description of some of the more common consistencies when it comes to cannabis extraction. It is also worth noting that these will be referred to frequently in Chapters Five to Ten, as when you begin to make your own concentrates, you will need to know which consistency you are trying to achieve.

SHATTER

Solvent based: Butane Oil is the most commonly used extractor

Process: It is specially treated to allow for it to cool without being agitated, and then kept at lower temperatures throughout processing. Terpenes and moisture are removed to increase the THC percentage.

Description: This is probably the more popular of the concentrates when smoked. Shatter is so named for its similarity to glass and tendency to 'shatter,' when dropped. It's often hard like glass, and even transparent too; although this transparency is a brown, honey colored glass. It's important to know that this color has no effect on the THC levels or purity of the product.

Although the way that it looks is often consistent, the texture of the shatter can change depending on (1) the concentrate used to make it and (2) the process it undergoes during extraction. It can be either tough and smooth to the touch, or softer and sticky; almost like taffy. Sometimes it can be snapped into pieces, while other times it bends and stretches when being broken.

The reason for its popularity is two-fold. One, it's easy to handle and store. For smokers especially, it's extremely easy to apply to a dab rig (see Chapter Three). The other reason for its popularity is that it is one of the more potent forms of concentrate, on account of the way that it is made.

WAX

<u>Solvent based</u>: Butane Oil is the most commonly used extractor

Process: The cannabis bud is placed in a specific vessel as the solvent is passed through it. This solvent is given space to evaporate, leaving only the oily essence of the plant behind. It is then purged; the process where residue solvents are removed.

Description: The term 'wax' can really be used to describe any of the softer consistencies when it comes to concentrates. It is almost always very sticky and oily, and quite often gooey as well. The important note here is that it is not runny; it's still technically a solid.

BUDDER

Solvent Based: Butane Oil is the most commonly used extractor

Process: Budder will most often start off as either an oil or wax. It is then whipped by hand, often over a low heat, to change the texture and consistency.

Description: The easiest way to think of budder is like peanut butter. If made correctly it will have the same thick and gooey consistency. It can still be just as pure as shatter can be, but the advantage, or common use, is the ease by which it can be turned into Cannabutter and eaten.

CRUMBLE

Solvent based: Butane Oil is the most commonly used extractor

Process: Crumble is made in a very similar way to that of shatter and budder, but the pre-purged oils used for crumble usually have more moisture, a different temperature and a thicker consistency. These factors help create the wax's crumbling, cheese-like body.

Description: Crumble is the direst consistency of all the solvent based concentrates. Depending on the solvents used and the process that it was made through, the crumble should be able to be broken into small pieces and 'crumbled' in your hand. Although, this often makes it very hard to handle too. It's not the preferred consistency when it comes to dabbing.

Don't Be Confused

One thing that I really need to mention before carrying into the next chapter, is that there is a lot of cross-over when it comes to concentrates. Above are a selection of some of the consistencies you will come across when sampling concentrates, but there are many others. Some are called by their consistency, others by their name. And what's more, some fall into both categories too. For example, bubble hash is technically a concentrate, but its consistency is so unique that it is referred to as such. And tincture is a liquid, but no one ever calls it that.

What you really need to be aware of is the solvents and extraction methods used. This is where the THC levels come from.

Chapter Four: Dabbing

Key Takeaway: *Dabbing and THC concentrates go together like peas and carrots. Dabbing is the process by which one smokes the cannabis extract. Because of the extreme heat needed to light the extract, a special 'dab' rig is used.*

What Is Dabbing?

A 'dab' is most commonly confused as a type of THC concentrate. More often than not, someone will say that they are having a 'dab,' when asked what they are smoking; rather than specifying what it is that they are actually ingesting. It's this ignorance that has led to the word also being interchangeable with actual concentrates. Well, to put it bluntly: it's not.

A 'dab,' or 'dabbing,' is an active noun that describes the process (one of many different processes) by which you are able to smoke the THC concentrate that you have made.

The main problem with cannabis extracts is that it is very hard to make them burn. Extreme heat needs to be applied to the concentrate to achieve the same affect that one would get with a lighter and a pipe. Dabbing is therefore the specific act of smoking extracts.

The Equipment

A quick note. As this book is about cannabis concentrates, primarily for medicinal purposes, I will not be going into great detail on dabbing. This is mainly a 'cover all bases' approach so that you have somewhere to start if you do wish to pursue dabbing.

The first thing you will need to dab is a dab rig. This is much like a bong, but instead of the glass bowl where you pack your weed, you have a male or female glass joint intended to hold a 'nail.' The nail is an extension piece where you pack your concentrate. It sits up at a vertical angle off the glass joint and comes in a variety of designs.

Next, you will need a dabber. A dabber is just a device that you use to transfer your concentrate from its storage unit to the end of the nail for smoking. And, finally, you need the torch. As a lighter doesn't get hot enough, a standard issue butane torch is used by most, although now an e-nail is becoming more popular. This is an electronically powered nail that heats itself to the desired temperature.

To actually 'dab' you need to heat the nail, place the concentrate on its end, leave it for roughly 10 seconds and then pull on the end of the rig as you would a bong.

The Pros And Cons Of Dabbing

The main pro behind dabbing comes from the concentrate itself, and that's the real point to take away from this. As the THC concentrate is so much more potent than natural bud, you will only need to use a very small amount per hit. This makes it a more economical way to smoke. Also, as it's pure THC, it is also believed to be better for you than smoking other strands.

The cons are primarily linked to danger. Where once the idea of overdosing on weed was seen as impossible, it's now a very real possibility. Because such a small amount of concentrate is needed to do the job, many first timers go too hard and risk 'over dosing.' Of course, this usually just means passing out, and getting a little nauseous, but it's still worth considering.

Also, the use of the butane torch can be extremely dangerous, especially when it comes to the heating of glass. Extreme caution is recommended here.

Chapter Five: How To Make Kief

Key Takeaway: *Kief is the most simple and easy to extract of all the concentrates. Unlike other extracts though it's rarely used on its own. Instead it's usually added to other weed products for an additional high.*

Other Names

Sift, Dry Sift.

Description

Kief is the simplest to make of all the concentrates. The chances are that if you are an avid user of cannabis you have already made it at one point and didn't even realize. So, what is it?

When you have a fully formed weed plant, trichomes form on the leaves and bud. If you look closely at your plant, you'll even be able to see them. These trichomes hold a vast majority of the cannabinoids that get you high (THC). The kief is the grounded down form of these cannabinoids, in their pure form.

Although its potency only tops out at about 60%, it's still very popular (especially when compared to the 15%-20% of normal bud) . The best way to ingest is to sprinkle it over the bud that you are about to smoke.

Solvent Used

None.

Consistency

It comes out looking like dust particles; sometimes clumped together.

How To Make

The collection process for kief is extremely simple and easy to do. There are more complex and effective ways to do this (see Chapter Six) but for now let's keep it simple with two.

One thing you are going to want to do before you begin your collection is put your bud in the freezer first; overnight should do. Doing this allows the trichomes to become solid and brittle. That way when you grind, more are likely to pass through, improving your yield.

METHOD ONE: BASIC KIEF GRIND

Equipment: A three-piece grinder

Time Spent: 30 seconds

All you need is a three (or four) piece grinder. The construction of these grinders allow for the ground herb (that which is going to be smoked) to be caught, while the left over kief trickles through the screen and is collected by the base. Simply put your bud in the grinder and grind away. The kief will collect itself.

METHOD TWO: DRY SIFT

Equipment: 2-3 micro-mesh screens, bins (containers), credit card

Time Spent: 15 – 30 minutes

1. You will want to place your micro-mesh screen above a 'bin,' or some sort of container to catch the kief and store your second screen. I recommend buying a bubble box for this.
2. Take one to two handfuls of weed and drop onto the top of the micro-mesh screen
3. Using your hands at first, lightly distress the weed plant. Don't break it purposefully, as this will limit the amount of kief you will yield. Just run your ran over it lightly, until it breaks up. This will take several minutes but by the end you

will notice that the weed no longer has any trichomes on top.
4. Once this is broken down, remove the top screen and on the second one you will see a pile of kief. Now, using your credit card, rake the kief back a forth over this second screen. This process will take a little longer and will end when all the kief is gone.
5. Lift up that screen and you will see a nice little pile of kief waiting for you. If you like you can repeat the process again with another screen.

Chapter Six: How To Make Hash

Key Takeaway: *Process is everything. If you want really good hash, rather than just ordinary kief, it is vital that you go through the few extra steps. It's always worth it.*

Other Names

Bubble Hash, Ice Water Hash, Full Melt.

Description

Hash comes in many different forms and consistencies. For the most part, hash is just a fancy word for kief. But more importantly, it's the way that the kief is extracted that really makes hash what it is. Above you will see a variety of names from bubble hash to full melt. These are all technically the same thing. The only change is the method via which they are collected.

Where bubble hash and others separate themselves from basic kief is the consistency. Good hash can get well into the 90% range, if done correctly.

Below I will detail the two best and simplest of methods to help you collect the best 'hash.' I will then provide you with a simple way to combine this hash into the solid block shape that you are probably familiar with.

Solvent Used

Ice water.

Consistency

Starts off in a fine, powdery dust form. When finished, it will be a hard block, like frozen cheese but also a little sticky.

How To Make

METHOD ONE: BLENDER

Using a blender is a great 'at home method' that you can try. It's based off the principle that trichomes are heavier than water and that by freezing them you will make them more solid and accessible for collection.

Equipment: A blender, sifter, paper coffee filters, one large jar, water, ice

Time Spent: 40 minutes waiting time, 15 minutes prep

1. Begin by placing your bud in the blender. No more than half full.

2. Then cover the bud with cold water and add a lot of ice cubes. The more that you can fit in the better.
3. Blend for about a minute. You should see the trichomes separate from the leaves and bus. This is a result of the ice, which literally whacks them off the plant.
4. Next, using the sifter, pour your mixture into a large glass jar. This will get rid of the plant material and just leave you with a greenish sludge water filled with trichomes.
5. Place the jar in the fridge for 30 minutes. Leave for longer, if needed. What you should see is the trichomes sink to the bottom.
6. Drain the jar by about two thirds. You can use a sieve for this, or just tip the jar while ensuring that the trichomes at the bottom don't come out.
7. Finally, put the jar in the freezer for about 10 minutes. Once this is done, pour the water through the coffee paper filter. The water will pass through and the trichomes will sit on top.

METHOD TWO: BUBBLE BAGS

Equipment: 7 bubble bags, 2 large plastic buckets, ice cubes, stainless steel skimming spoon, oil pads.

Time Spent: 15 minutes

1. In bucket number one, stack six of your bubble bags. Do this by putting one in flat, then putting the other into that one and so on. What you are doing is creating a filtration system. This works best if you buy 6 different sized bags.
2. In bucket number two put the seventh bubble bag. Next, fill this bucket halfway with water, ice and your weed. Allow to soak for up to ten minutes. The idea is to get the weed as cold as possible, so a little extra time isn't a bad thing.
3. Using your spoon, stir the mixture for about five minutes. Don't be afraid to mix with a little force, you're trying to knock the trichomes off the flower.

4. Next, lift the ice water bubble bag up and let it drain into the bottom of the bucket. What you should be holding is a bubble bag full of mashed up weed, ice and a little water.
5. Now, pour that mixture into bucket with the six bags, slowly allowing all the water to drain. At the base of each bag, you should see a collection of either hash or weed extract. The bottom three bags should yield the most hash.
6. Pour this onto a flat surface and allow to dry.

METHOD THREE: CREATING THE HASH BLOCKS

Equipment: cellophane wrap, paper, tape, rolling pin, oven

Time Spent: 10 minutes waiting time, 5 minutes prep

1. Wrap the kief in cellophane, kind of the same way that you would wrap a sandwich. It needs to be firm, tight and most importantly, waterproof.

2. Take this wrapping and wrap it up in paper. Then tape it shut. Try and keep it all as firm as possible.
3. Run the package under water, so that the entire thing is completely wet.
4. Heat the oven to 350°F and cook the kief for ten minutes. The water will ensure that nothing is burned.
5. Take the package out of the oven and place on a flat, hard surface.
6. Next you will need to use a rolling pin and literally roll the package with all the force that you can. Make sure that you roll evenly from all sides.
7. After several minutes of this, open the package and check the consistency. If it is still crumbly and not compact, repeat steps 1-6.
8. It will be done when the hash is moulded together into a firm substance.

Chapter Seven: How To Make Cannabutter

Key Takeaway*: Cannabutter is one of the more common THC extracts. The reason for this is that it's so simple to make and can be added to almost any meal for a nice body high.*

Other Names

Bud butter, Cannabis butter, Budder.

Description

In Chapter Three, I spoke of 'Budder.' This is as different from Cannabutter as it is the same. What does that mean? Allow me to explain.

In this chapter, you will learn how to make at home, edible Cannabutter. This is essentially the process of using butter to extract the THC from the weed plant. In that sense, it is a budder, plain and true.

The difference between the two (Cannabutter and budder) lies in the solvent used. Here, butter and water are used for extraction. For stronger forms of budder, it's often suggested to make a shatter or wax with butane first, and then transform it into budder through whipping and manipulation. But I prefer this method as it's easier and more delicious.

Solvent Used

Water, butter.

Consistency

A creamy, butter like consistency

How To Make

There are two processes that you can use when making cannabutter; that is with either a stove top or a slow cooker. Here I will detail both.

Note: The first thing you must do before beginning either method is heat the weed that you are going to use. You can use a stove top or oven for this. I like to put my weed in the oven at 175°F for 30 minutes. Heating the weed will put it through a decarboxylate process. What this essentially does is activate the THC ingredient in the weed, much the same as when you use a lighter to smoke it. This will give you a far more potent yield.

METHOD ONE: STOVE TOP

Equipment: 1 pound unsalted butter, 1 cup water, 1 ounce of weed (ground), mesh strainer

Time Spent: 2-3 hours waiting time, 15 minutes prep

1. On a low heat, add the butter and water into a pan and stir.
2. Mix slowly until the butter begins to melt.
3. Pour the ground weed into the mixture and continue to stir. Make sure that the mixture never comes to a full boil.
4. Maintain a low heat and let the mix simmer for 2-3 hours. Just know that if you cook for too long, the flavor will start to become bitter as the heat may extract more chlorophyll and alkaloids from the plant than is necessary.
5. Pour the mixture through a mesh strainer so that all the leaves and plant products are extracted. This should leave just the trichomes behind.
6. Place the mixture in the fridge overnight. The next day you should see the butter separate from the water. Discard the water and keep the butter.

METHOD TWO: SLOW COOKER

Equipment: 1 pound unsalted butter, 1 cup water, 1 ounce of weed (ground), mesh strainer.

Time Spent: 10-24 hours waiting time.

1. Turn the slow cooker onto a low heat.
2. Add the water, butter and weed.
3. Allow to cook for anywhere between 10-24 hours. The longer you leave it, the more infused the cannabinoids will be with the butter.
4. Pour the mixture through a mesh strainer, so that all the leaves and plant products are extracted. This should leave just the trichomes behind.
5. Place the mixture in the fridge overnight. The next day you should see the butter separate from the water. Discard the water and keep the butter.

Chapter Eight: How To Make Rosin

Key Takeaway: *The best way to think about Rosin is like juice from the bud. Although it is relatively new on the market, its simple formula has made it one of the more popular methods of extraction.*

In this chapter, you will learn the very simple art of making Rosin, one of the simplest extracts to make.

Description

Rosin is essentially the resin of the flower from you cannabis plant, pushed out via heat and pressure. Over the last few years it has been gaining a lot of popularity due to how extremely easy it is to extract. With the exception of basic kief, it is perhaps the easiest of the extracts to get your hands on.

The only real downside to this method is that the yield isn't as high as some other forms of extracts. Although it is indeed easy, it will only get you a 50%-70% potency level.

Solvent Used

None. Heat and pressure only.

Consistency

When you press the Rosin out initially, it will be an oil. However, once collected and cooled down, it becomes more of a wax, like tree sap. Very stick.y

How To Make

The process that I am going to use is called Rosin tech. It employs the use of a hair straightener, but any device you have that works in the same way will do the job e.g. two hot irons pressed together.

Furthermore, make sure that the flower that you are using is moist and sticky. The drier the flower, the less yield you will produce and you don't want that.

Equipment: Hair straightener, parchment paper, metal scraper.

Time Spent: 2 minutes.

1. Place your cannabis flower in the center of your parchment paper. The parchment paper only has to be large enough to fold over the flower.
2. Pre-heat your hair straightener. Not too hot though, keep it on the lowest setting.
3. Use your fingers to flatten the weed out in the paper by pressing down lightly.
4. Place the paper in the center of the hair straightener tongs. Ensure that all of the weed will be covered by the tongs when you press down.
5. Close the hair straightener, applying pressure so as to squash the weed. flower. The more

pressure, the better. Think of this like juicing; you're literally juicing the resin from the flower.
6. Press down for only a handful of seconds (2-4).
7. Open the paper and you should see golden brown resin oil. Use the metal scraper to collect.

Chapter Nine: How To Make Tinctures

Key Takeaway: Tinctures are without a doubt the best options for a person who requires the medicinal properties of marijuana, but doesn't want to smoke. It's simple to make and even more simple to take.

Other Names

Green dragon.

Description

In the biological world, a tincture is a medicine made by dissolving a plant in alcohol. This extracts the necessary properties from the plant, allowing for you to consume it more freely. Cannabis tinctures work on the same principle. Using alcohol, the cannabinoids are extracted from the plant, leaving you with THC infused alcohol.

The main advantage to this is ease of use. Most people will store their tincture in an eye dropper of sorts, allowing for them to distribute the tincture in small dosages as they see fit. And the great thing about tincture is, like any extract, you only need a small amount. Up to five drops under your tongue will induce a body high far quicker and easier than any amount of weed brownies ever could.

Another advantage, of course, is that it is a smokeless process. The tincture is especially popular for patients who rely on THC for its medicinal purposes, but don't want to smoke.

Solvent Used

Alcohol.

Consistency

It comes out as a liquid, much like the alcohol it was extracted with.

How To Make

This process is for a person using bud. The dosages per 500 ml of alcohol will change depending on the source that you use. Below, I will provide the measurements needed for other cannabis sources.

Also, as with making the cannabutter, you will want to decarboxylate (heat up) your bud before starting. The easiest way to do this is in an oven at 240°F for 30 minutes.

Equipment: 1 ounce bud (chopped), 500 ml 95% Grain alcohol (or higher), coffee filters, three mason jars, strainer, glass bowl, saucepan, thermometer.

Time Spent: 1 hour to make, 4-5 days to prepare.

Cannabis Source:

- Bud – 1 ounce
- Leaf – 3 to 4 ounces
- Trim – 2 ounces
- Hash – 6 to 8 grams

1. Your bud should be chopped. Now place it in one of the mason jars.
2. Pour the 500ml of alcohol over the weed. It should just cover the top of your weed.
3. Close the jar off and shake it as hard as you can. Place the jar in the freezer.
4. Over the next 4-5 days, remove the jar from the freezer twice a day and give it another good shake.
5. Once ready, pour the mixture through the strainer into another jar. This will leave you with just the liquid.
6. Using the coffee filters (double stacked), again strain the mixture into a third mason jar. This

will take a while, but will leave you with very pure liquid.

7. Fill the saucepan with water and bring it to boil on the stove. Place the glass bowl over the boiling water. What you are doing is creating a double boiler, so it's important that the glass bowl sits in the water.
8. Pour the strained liquid into the glass bowl and begin to stir.
9. Using the thermometer, make sure that the liquid stays between 150°F and 170°F.
10. Stir for 45 minutes. When you are done, the liquid will have dissolved to about 1/3 of its original volume.
11. Pour into a clean mason jar and leave it in the freezer over-night. This will allow the fats and lipids to separate from the tincture, leaving you with a much more refined product.
12. Enjoy!

Chapter Ten: How To Make RSO (Rick Simpson Oil)

Key Takeaway*: This is another great extract with medicinal purposes. Although it's a little more complex to make than others, it's amazing for skin damage and again, doesn't need to be smoked.*

Description

Rick Simpson Oil originates from its namesake, Rick Simpson. In 2003, Rick Simpson discovered a series of cancerous spots on his skin. When surgery failed, he turned to medicinal marijuana remedies, in particular oils and solvents. Making his own oil through well-known extraction techniques, he applied it to his skin and within days began to see the cancer healing. Since then, he has dedicated his life to spreading the word of marijuana healing properties, being responsible for the healing of over 5000 cancer victims.

Rick Simpson Oil is different to a lot of other extracts as it isn't ingested, rather applied on the skin. The amount to apply changes per person and maladies, and a medical professional's advice should be sought before using it yourself.

The potency of Rick Simpson Oil can also get quite high. Although it ultimately depends on the cannabis being used, it can reach levels as high as 60% - 90%.

Solvent Used

99% Isopropyl alcohol is best.

Consistency

It varies between a wax and an oil. Soft and runny enough that it can be easily spread onto the skin.

Warning

Before you do attempt to make Rick Simpson Oil at home, be warned that it is an extremely dangerous process. Not only are the solvents extremely flammable, but they are also prone to explode if treated the wrong way. Avoid smoke, sparks, stove tops and heat guns. And also make sure that when you do make the oil, that you do it in a well-ventilated room or outdoors.

How To Make

This process is based on the process described on the Rick Simpson website. It is by far the most efficient, easiest and safest method to make the oil.

Also, as with making the cannabutter, you will want to decarboxylate (heat up) your bud before starting. The easiest way to do this is in an oven at 240°F for 30 minutes.

This process, if you use the measurements specified, will yield you roughly 3-4 grams of oil.

Equipment: 1 ounce bud, 500ml 99% ISO alcohol, 1 mixing stick, two large jars, 1 small rice cooker, a fan, coffee filters, 1 plastic bag, oven mits, small stainless steel container, coffee warmer

1. I like to start slow by adding my bud to a plastic bag and pouring a few splashes of my solvent into the bag. Using your hands on the outside of the bag, crush the bud up with the solvent.
2. Add the contents to a jar and pour the rest of the solvent in with it.
3. Using a mixing stick, mix and crush the bud up with the solvent. Mix for about three minutes, until the plant is fully crushed and mixed.
4. Pour this solvent mixture through a coffee filter into the second large jar. I like to double up on the filters to ensure that I get the purest product.
5. For this next part make sure that you are in a well-ventilated room. Use the fan if required.

6. Turn the rice cooker on to a high heat and add the solvent mixture to the cooker. Bring the mixture to the boil.
7. Only fill the cooker to about 2/3 full. If you have more mixture than can fit in the cooker than that's OK. As the mixture evaporates, slowly add more solvent.
8. As the mixture begins to evaporate for the last time (when there is no more solvent left to add) add 5 – 10 drops of water into the mixture. This will help to release the solvent residue.
9. When there's about an inch left of solvent, put on your oven mits and lift the cooker off the heat. Swirl the container and its contents slowly until the solvent has finished boiling off.
10. Pour the solvent into the small stainless steel container.
11. Put the stainless steel container in the coffee warmer and leave it. The idea here is for the remaining water residue to slowly evaporate off the oil, leaving you with nothing but product. It may take a few hours, but when done you will

have a dark, honey brown oil that can be easily applied to your skin.

Final Thoughts

Another congratulation is in order, I think!

If you're reading this than I assume that you have read the entire book and hopefully tried a few of the methods out for yourself. I really hope that by now you are beginning to see the benefits of using extracts over pure bud. From a medicinal standpoint, the effects are far superior and easier to achieve.

But now that you have finished the book, you're probably wondering where to go from here? My advice is to start to experiment. I compared this book to a cookbook earlier for a good reason. Now that you know the basics behind extraction and how to get the most from each process, it's worth experimenting and trying new things. If you like one method more than the others, try and perfect and build upon it. By no means are the methods I present perfect or the only way.

And also, spread the knowledge. To me that's always been the most important thing. You were probably skeptical about the use of cannabis extracts before you bought this book. But now that you have been able to try it, you can't believe that it took so long to get on board! So, to that I say you owe it to yourself to tell your friends and share your knowledge.

And finally, when it's all said and done, I want to again say thank you. I truly do hope that in reading this book you learned a few things and most importantly had fun.

BONUS CHAPTER: What Is CBD?

This is a bonus chapter from my book '**CBD Hemp Oil 101**: *The Essential Beginner's Guide To CBD and Hemp Oil to Improve Health, Reduce Pain and Anxiety, and Cure Illnesses.*' Enjoy!

***

Key Takeaway: *Negative perception regarding cannabidiol continues to decline, particularly as its positive effects are unmasked. What exactly is this compound and why is it becoming the next big thing among those looking for natural treatments?*

Cannabidiol or CBD is a chemical compound found in the cannabis plant. The plant itself contains about 113 active cannabinoids, and cannabidiol is considered a major phytocannabinoid making up about 40% of the cannabis plant's extract.

In recent years, scientific studies have shown the many medicinal effects of cannabidiol. Moreover, its nonpsychoactive characteristics and lack of interference with psychological and psychomotor functions have also been extolled by researchers.

When the subject is cannabis, most people associate it with the widely popular use of the plant as a recreational drug. Hence, compounds in the plant such as cannabidiol are immediately viewed as potentially inducing a feeling of being "high". However, cannabidiol does not cause this feeling in users at all! Rather, it has been shown to all the following effects:

- anti-inflammatory
- antioxidant
- analgesic
- antidepressant
- anti-tumoral

- anti-psychotic, and
- anxiolytic.

Cannabinoid Cell Receptors

Cannabidiol is found mostly inside the resin glands or trichomes of cannabis. CBD, along with other cannabinoids in the plant, binds itself to the cells' cannabinoid receptors, which are primarily found in the body's central nervous system as well as other organs, including the skin, digestive system, and the reproductive organs. The body's cell receptors collectively form a network called the endocannabinoid system.

Endocannabinoid System (ECS)

The endocannabinoid system or ECS is a neurotransmitter system responsible for many regular body functions and feelings, including:

- memory

- motor control
- mood
- reproduction
- immune function
- appetite
- sleep
- pain reception, and
- bone development.

The ECS also regulates the body's energy balance or homeostatic functions. When ingested, cannabinoid appears to interact with the body's ECS, causing the therapeutic effects reported by users of CBD Hemp Oil and other CBD products.

How CBD differs from THC

Cannabidiol is different from another compound also found in the cannabis plant, tetrahydrocannabinol or THC.

THC is the major psychoactive agent in cannabis, and is mainly responsible for that "high" that cannabis users experience when using cannabis recreationally. THC's side effects include:

- lethargy
- decrease in body coordination
- postural hypotension, and
- slurred speech.

Others may also experience hallucinations, mood swings, behavioral changes, paranoia, dizziness, fatigue, or feelings of inebriation when ingesting THC.

That is not to say that THC has not been researched or utilized for medicinal or scientific purposes as well. THC has been formulated into dronabinol and is available by prescription in the United States and Canada, among other countries. Dronabinol is currently being used to treat anorexia or other eating disorders in HIV/AIDS patients, and to control nausea or vomiting experienced by cancer patients who are undergoing chemotherapy.

THC is also an active ingredient in nabiximols, a botanical drug prescribed for people suffering from multiple sclerosis. This drug was approved in the United Kingdom in 2010 to relieve neuropathic pain, overactive bladder function, spasticity, and other effects of multiple sclerosis.

So, THC and CBD both interact with the body's cellular receptors, but the effects are markedly different. Aside from the lack of psychoactive effects in CBD, it also

- balances out or counteract anxiety.
- has antipsychotic effects, unlike THC which can trigger or exacerbate psychosis or hallucinations.
- has – perhaps the most noteworthy – a positive effect on wakefulness.

The Case For CBD: Charlotte's Web

Cannabidiol and its medicinal use broke into mainstream consciousness in 2013, when the case of a baby named Charlotte Figi made headlines. Charlotte, along with her twin Chase, was born October 18, 2006 to Matt and Paige Figi. The twins were born perfectly healthy, but after a few months it became apparent that Charlotte was suffering from a medical condition of some sort.

One day, Charlotte suddenly started having a seizure. She was laying on her back on the floor, with flickering eyes. That first seizure lasted about half an hour, and Matt and Paige rushed their baby to the hospital.

In a CNN article that covered the story, Paige recalled that they weren't calling it epilepsy. They thought it was just a random seizure. They examined Charlotte in every possible way (MRI, EEG, etc.), but found nothing. Ultimately, they were sent home.

However, over the next few weeks, Charlotte would continue to get seizures, some often lasting two to four hours. Hospital tests could not find anything, and the doctors could not figure out what was going on. "*They said it's probably going to go away,*" Paige said. "*It is unusual in that it's so severe, but it's probably something she'll grow out of.*"

After many more tests and frequent seizures, a doctor diagnosed Charlotte with a rare intractable epilepsy called Dravet Syndrome. This form of epilepsy is different in that the epileptic seizures cannot be controlled by any medication. Charlotte was being treated with seven types of drugs, including barbiturates and benzodiazepines, but the seizures were still occurring.

"*At 2, she really started to decline cognitively,*" Paige said. "*Whether it was the medicines or the seizures, it was happening, it was obvious. And she was slipping away.*"

They also took Charlotte to a Dravet specialist in Chicago who recommended a ketogenic diet, high-fat and low-carb, used mostly for epilepsy patients. The diet induces the body to produce more ketones which are the body's natural chemicals against seizures. The diet controlled Charlotte's seizures, but not without adverse side effects such as bone loss, compromised immune system, and even behavioral effects.

When her parents saw her eating pine cones and other stuff outside, they asked themselves: is this treatment, with all its unpleasant side effects, truly beneficial?

Matt was desperate, and he began researching online for other possible solutions. He found an online video showing a boy in California also diagnosed with Dravet Syndrome and being treated using a strain of cannabis that was low in THC and high in CBD. The treatment was working to control his seizures.

Charlotte was already five years old around this time, and Colorado had only recently approved medical marijuana. Matt and Paige decided it was worth a shot, but they needed two doctors to sign off on their daughter's medical marijuana card.

After receiving countless rejections, they finally got in touch with Dr. Margaret Gedde, who agreed to meet with them. Even though Charlotte would have been the youngest in the state to apply for the card.

Dr. Gedde signed off on Charlotte's medical marijuana card. "*Charlotte's been close to death so many times, she's had so much brain damage from seizure activity and likely the pharmaceutical medication,*" Gedde said. "*When you put the potential risks of the cannabis in context like that, it's a very easy decision.*"

Another doctor, Alan Shackelford, was hesitant because of Charlotte's age, but eventually signed off because of the desperate situation. He felt that all other treatment options had been exhausted, and cannabis was their only remaining option.

They located a marijuana dispensary in Denver selling a strain called R4, with very low THC and high CBD. A friend extracted the CBD oil from the cannabis, and after the oil was tested at a local laboratory, they began treating Charlotte with small doses.

"We were pioneering the whole thing; we were guinea pigging Charlotte," according to Paige. *"This is a federally illegal substance. I was terrified to be honest with you."*

Matt and Paige were very surprised at the results. Charlotte didn't have any seizures in the first hour, which was a positive first sign. And it just got better after that: the seizures were gone in about a week!

Charlotte's health has improved, and the seizures have become very infrequent, mostly happening only while she is sleeping. She has become physically active, being able to walk, ride a bicycle, and feed herself.

"I didn't hear her laugh for six months," Paige said. *"I didn't hear her voice at all, just her crying. I can't imagine that I would be watching her making these gains that she's making, doing the things that she's doing (without the medical marijuana). I don't take it for granted. Every day is a blessing."*

The strain of marijuana that Matt and Paige used for Charlotte is now called Charlotte's Web, and is being used by many other patients suffering from cancer, epilepsy, and other diseases.

Because of Charlotte's story, the spotlight has now been focused on CBD. Over the next few chapters, let's look at more characteristics of cannabidiol and why it is being regarded as a miracle compound.

***

This is the end of this bonus chapter.

Want to continue reading?

Then get your copy of "CBD Hemp Oil 101" at your favorite bookstore!

Did You Like This Book?

If you enjoyed this book, I would like to ask you for a favor. Would you be kind enough to share your thoughts and post a review of this book? Just a few sentences would already be really helpful.

Your voice is important for this book to reach as many people as possible.

The more reviews this book gets, the more people will be able to find it and learn how they can make their own cannabis extracts.

Thank you again for reading this book and good luck with applying everything you have learned!

I'm rooting for you...

By The Same Author

AQUAPONICS 101

THE EASY BEGINNER'S GUIDE TO AQUAPONIC GARDENING:
How To Build Your Own Backyard Aquaponics System
& Grow Organic Vegetables With Hydroponics And Fish

TOMMY ROSENTHAL

HYDROPONICS 101

THE EASY BEGINNER'S GUIDE TO HYDROPONIC GARDENING:
Learn How To Build a Backyard Hydroponics System
for Homegrown Organic Fruit, Herbs and Vegetables

TOMMY ROSENTHAL

CPSIA information can be obtained
at www.ICGtesting.com
Printed in the USA
BVHW070909080221
599618BV00015B/1029